Eating Apples

by

Gail Saunders-Smith

Pebble Books

an imprint of Capstone Press

Pebble Books are published by Capstone Press
151 Good Counsel Drive, P.O. Box 669, Mankato, Minnesota 56002
http://www.capstone-press.com

Printed in the United States of America

2 3 4 5 6 7 07 06 05 04 03

Library of Congress Cataloging-in-Publication Data
Saunders-Smith, Gail.
Eating Apples / by Gail Saunders-Smith.
p. cm.—(Apples)
Summary: Photographs and simple text describe different ways to enjoy apples--whole, sliced, cooked, and juiced.
ISBN 1-56065-582-8 (hardcover)
ISBN 1-56065-950-5 (paperback)1. Goats—Juvenile literature. [1. Goats.] I. Title. II. Series.
TX813.A6S28 1998
641.6'411—dc21 97-29799

Editorial Credits
Lois Wallentine, editor; Timothy Halldin and James Franklin, design; Michelle L. Norstad, photo research

Photo Credits
Michelle Coughlan, 1, 4, 8, 12, 14
Unicorn Stock/Jean Higgins, cover; Paul A. Hein, 6; Doris Brookes, 10; David Cummings, 16; Pamela Pruett-Power, 18; Chuck Schmeiser, 20

Table of Contents

Raw Apples 5
Cooked Apples 9
Liquid Apples 15
Fun Apples 19

Words to Know 22
Read More 23
Internet Sites 23
Index/Word List 24

apples

apple slices

apple pie

apple crisp

apple sauce

apple juice

apple cider

caramel apple

apple fun

Words to Know

caramel—a candy made from burnt sugar, butter, and milk; caramel is sometimes used to coat whole apples.

cider—a drink made from pressed apples

crisp—a dessert made from fruit and a crumbled crust

juice—a drink made from the liquid of fruit or vegetables

pie—a dessert made from fruit and a pastry crust

sauce—fruit that is cooked until soft

Read More

Burckhardt, Ann L. *Apples.* Mankato, Minn.: Bridgestone Books, 1996.

Gibbons, Gail. *The Seasons of Arnold's Apple Tree.* San Diego: Harcourt Brace Jovanovich, 1984.

Micucci, Charles. *The Life and Times of the Apple.* New York: Orchard Books, 1992.

Internet Sites

Do you want to find out more about apples? Let FactHound, our fact-finding hound dog, do the research for you.

Here's how:

1) Visit ***http://www.facthound.com***

2) Type in the **Book ID** number: **1560655828**

3) Click on **FETCH IT**.

FactHound will fetch Internet sites picked by our editors just for you!

Note to Parents and Teachers

The Apple series supports national science standards on units on nutrition. This book describes and illustrates types of food made from apples. The photographs support early readers understanding of the text. The repetition of words and phrases helps early readers learn new words. This book also introduces early readers to subject-specific vocabulary words, which are defined in the Words to Know section. Early readers may need assistance to read some words and to use the Table of Contents, Words to Know, Read More, Internet Sites, and Index/Word list sections of the book.

Index/Word List

apple, 5, 7, 9, 11, 13, 15, 17, 19, 21
caramel, 19
cider, 17
crisp, 11
fun, 21
juice, 15
pie, 9
sauce, 13
slices, 7

Word Count: 17
Early-Intervention Level: 3

W